My Way West

Real Kids Traveling the Oregon & California Trails

Written & Illustrated by
Elizabeth Goss

WEST
MARGIN
PRESS

EMIGRATION!
OREGON
CALIFORNIA

"Although I was but a girl of 11 years, I distinctly remember many things connected with that far-off time when all our western country was a wilderness." —*Etty Scott, age 11*

THE JOURNEY WEST

How do you pull a horse out of quicksand? Can you cook beans in a hot spring? What does bread made from crickets and acorns taste like? Between 1841 and 1884 around 40,000 young people discovered the answers to unusual questions like these.

They were part of the Westward Expansion, a move to extend the United States into the land west of the Mississippi River. These emigrants, also called overlanders, used over-land routes like the Oregon and California Trails to travel west across North America. They crossed windy prairies and scorching deserts, wild rivers and icy mountains, hoping to make new homes in places they had never seen before.

These young emigrants were ordinary people. They played games and had favorite foods. They loved and took care of their pets. They bothered their siblings and played pranks on their friends. But they also did extraordinary things. Emigrant children drove ox teams and caught runaway cattle. They walked barefoot through snow and over cactus. They kept traveling even when it seemed impossible.

The westward trails were unpredictable and challenging. Some emigrants enjoyed fairly uneventful trips full of music, stargazing, and jaw-dropping scenery. Others seemed to meet only bad luck and tragedy. For most, the journey was a blend of good fortune and bad.

Young overlanders started out from different states and even different countries. They spoke different languages and practiced different religions. Some traveled with plenty of supplies. Others had barely enough to survive. But they all did their best to help their families journey west.

"And what is the harm in simply penning a few thoughts now and then by the side of the way, for it is a new and strange way that we are going to travel." —*Harriet Hitchcock, age 13*

"I was a small child when the first white people came into our country. They came like a lion, yes, like a roaring lion, and have continued so ever since, and I have never forgotten their first coming."
—*Thocmetony, Northern Paiute, age 10*

THE LAND WAS NOT EMPTY

The overlanders often talked about the West as if it were an empty place with no one living in it. But Native American communities had thrived across North America for thousands of years. The land the emigrants traveled through, and wanted to claim, was already home to hundreds of unique nations of people with their own governments, languages, and traditions.

Ohiyesa, of the Santee Sioux Nation, remembered the happiness of his childhood vividly. "To me, as a boy, this wilderness was a paradise." He went hunting with his friends, made maple sugar with his grandmother, and learned the history and stories of his people. But he also remembered hardships like going without food during a hard spring, and fleeing from the violent conflicts between the Santee Sioux and the "Big Knives," the white people.

For emigrant children, being part of the Westward Expansion was a chance for a better life. But for young Native Americans, it meant something devastating. They faced the destruction of their homes and families, and the loss of their cultures, customs, and sometimes their very lives.

The land in the West was advertised to the overlanders as free. But the Westward Expansion had a staggering cost to the people who were already living in the West. The overlanders set out on the westward trails with great hopes for what the journey might bring them and without a care for what it brought the Native Americans.

As more and more emigrants decided to take the journey and change their lives, the lives of Native people changed too. And not for the better.

"The greatest object of their lives seems to be to acquire possessions—to be rich. They desire to possess the whole world."
—*Ohiyesa, Santee Sioux, age 8*

THE DECISION

The decision to move west was a life-changing one. Young emigrants left behind their relatives, best friends, and favorite pets—usually forever. Yet, they had little say in the decision to go. Parents, especially fathers, made the choice for the whole family. Young overlanders were often deeply sad about leaving home, even if they were also excited or curious about life in the West.

Land, gold, fresh starts, new freedoms, the adventure of a lifetime—the West seemed to offer endless possibilities. Many parents especially hoped the move would mean better health for their families. There was supposed to be little sickness out West, especially compared to crowded eastern cities.

"My mother is heartbroken over this separation of relatives and friends. Giving up old associations for what? Good health, perhaps." —*Sallie Hester, age 14*

Owen's father was a free African American and his mother was white. The family left a successful business in Missouri, believing that Oregon would be a fairer and freer place for them to live. —*Owen Bush, age 12*

Free African American emigrants hoped the West would offer all these things as well as relief from prejudice. Racist laws in the United States restricted where and how free African American families could live and failed to protect their rights. They believed the West would offer more freedom, opportunity, and safety than their eastern homes had.

Enslaved people were not allowed to choose if they wanted to move. If their white owners decided to take them west, enslaved Black people were forced to leave their loved ones behind and help their owners on the journey. They hoped to be freed at the trail's end. Slavery was illegal in Oregon and California, though that did not always translate to freedom.

Once emigrants made the decision to go west, they had to start getting ready. It took a lot of preparation to move across the country.

"The thing that decided [Father] to come to Oregon was he had heard there were plenty of fish here." —Benjamin Bonney, age 7

Ellen was born into slavery. When Ellen's slave owner decided to move, he took Ellen, her mother, and her younger sisters with him. —Ellen Mason, age 13

SUPPLIES

In many ways, deciding to go west was the easy part. It could take months to save money and make or buy what was needed for the trip. *The Emigrant's Guide To Oregon and California*, published in 1845, recommended that each adult bring "at least, two hundred pounds of flour, or meal; one hundred and fifty pounds of bacon; ten pounds of coffee; twenty pounds of sugar; and ten pounds of salt."

The guidebook also recommended packing things like a frying pan, a gun, tin plates and cups, blankets, a coffee pot, simple tools like hoes and spades, and beads and fishhooks to trade with Native Americans. The guide definitely did not recommend bringing things like delicate china, full libraries, or fancy furniture.

Overpacking may seem like a small mistake, but it was dangerous. The emigrants needed to reach the west side of the Rocky Mountains before

"[Father] had made over a hundred pounds of maple sugar the preceding fall which we took along instead of loaf sugar. He also took along plenty of cornmeal."
—*Benjamin Bonney, age 7*

"We had boxes of dried apples and peaches, tin pails of preserves, shortening for pie-crust and bread . . . some homemade bacon is very important." —*Jinny Watson, age 9*

winter. Speedy travel was vital. But overloaded oxen and mules moved slowly and grew tired easily. The guide's recommended food weighed 390 pounds on its own, but many overlanders still piled extra things like stoves and grandfather clocks into their wagons.

The cost of supplies added up quickly. Prices varied, but in 1859, it would have cost a family of four at least $500 to buy all the recommended gear to go west. That's more than $15,000 in today's money. Some families spent much more.

Many people could not afford these steep costs. Some people borrowed supplies from friends or family. Others made what they needed or went without important items. Some even went without a covered wagon.

"We have a cooking stove made of sheet iron, a portable table, tin plates and cups, cheap knives and forks (best ones packed away), camp stools, etc." —*Sallie Hester, age 14*

"Knowing that books were always scarce in a new country, we also took a good library of standard works." —*Virginia Reed, age 13*

WAGONS

Nicknamed Prairie Schooners because their canvas covers looked like the sails of ships, the covered wagons used by the emigrants were lightweight and tough. They were made mostly of wood and their bottoms could be waterproofed with tar or paint. Their few metal pieces, like the iron rings around the wheels, held the wagon together and protected wooden parts that could wear out easily.

The average Prairie Schooner was simple and built to get supplies across the country. But not all covered wagons were so practical. Some wealthy emigrants had dozens of wagons specially made to take their families and belongings west. Virginia Reed's family's wagons were all "made to order" and very luxurious. The one her mother rode in had two levels and a built-in stove with a chimney!

Many emigrant families could not afford to have a wagon made for them. They either had to build their own or fix up a farm wagon. Or go without. Some poor emigrant families on the Mormon Trail used handcarts on their journey to Utah. Parents often pulled or pushed the large two-wheeled handcart together. Older children also helped. These emigrants had to be extremely careful not to overpack or else the carts would become too heavy for them to move.

Mary Ann Stucki, a young handcart emigrant, remembered, "Mother was forced to leave behind her feather bed, the bolt of linen, two large trunks full of clothes, and some other valuable things which we needed so badly later."

"My father put in his spare time for some months making a strong sturdy wagon in which to cross the plains." —*Benjamin Bonney, age 7*

"My mother loaded all her worldly possessions, consisting of a stock of provisions and a camp outfit, into a canvas-covered wagon." —*Elisha Brooks, age 11*

"After preparing food and clothing, wagons came next. Father had his wagons made in Springfield, they were much larger and heavier wagons. They were to live in."
—*Jinny Watson, age 9*

"The men set to work making handcarts and my father, being a carpenter, helped make thirty-three of them. Ours was a small two-wheeled vehicle with two shafts and a cover on top." —*Mary Ann Stucki, age 6*

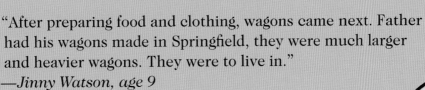

ANIMALS

Thousands of animals trekked the Western trails beside their humans. The ones that pulled the wagons were the most important. Some emigrants insisted that mules were the best beasts for the job. They did not frighten as easily as horses and moved faster than oxen.

Guidebooks recommended oxen because they were extremely strong and could handle months of hard work. Oxen also cost less than horses or mules and needed less food. In a pinch, however, emigrants would use any animal they could to pull their wagons, including milk cows.

Cattle and small farm animals like chickens were a good source of food on the trail. They could also be sold or traded for supplies out West. Ponies and horses helped the overlanders keep their herds of cattle together and scout ahead of the slow-moving wagons.

When it came to family pets, the emigrants faced a painful choice: bring their beloved animals with them on the unpredictable journey or leave them behind. Some families could not afford to feed and care for their animal friends as they traveled. Others worried that their pets would get lost or be attacked by wild creatures. Many overlanders chose to leave their pets behind with friends or relatives.

But others brought dogs, cats, and even pet birds with them on the trails. Some young travelers picked up new pets. They adopted stray dogs and baby calves, and even tamed wild animals like antelope and prairie dogs.

"The family wagon was drawn by four yoke of oxen... The other wagons were drawn by three yoke each. We had saddle horses and cows, and last but not least my pony. He was a beauty and his name was Billy." —*Virginia Reed, age 13*

"Two cows were also taken to provide milk and two laying hens in a coop at the tail end of the wagon." —*Elisha Brooks, age 11*

"We looked back and saw our old watchdog (his name was Watch) howling on the distant shore. Father had driven him back saying, 'Go back to Grandfather, Watch!'" —*Etty Scott, age 11*

"Lucy and I have caught [a prairie dog] and got it in a cage." —*Harriet Hitchcock, age 13*

"Many neighbors gathered in to bid us goodbye and many tears were shed as they gave the last handshakes."
—*Catherine Sager, age 9*

"My father started with our wagons one month in advance to St. Joseph, Missouri, our starting point."
—*Sallie Hester, age 14*

SETTING OUT & JUMPING OFF

Choosing the best time to leave could be tricky. *The Emigrant's Guide To Oregon and California* recommended starting out on the westward trails by May first: "Unless you pass over the mountains early in the fall, you are very liable to be detained by impossible mountains of snow, until next spring, or perhaps forever."

Setting out too early had drawbacks too. There might not be enough grass for the animals to eat yet and spring snowstorms could be dangerous. Elisha Brooks remembered another downside of leaving in early spring: "There was mud, mud everywhere—slush to drive through, to eat in, to sleep in."

Leaving for the West was a major event. Family and friends, and sometimes whole towns, might gather to watch a departure. Some communities sent their travelers off with cheers and parties. Others begged them to stay even as the wagons rolled away. As they watched their homes fade into the distance, many young emigrants felt a blend of excitement and sorrow. For most, this was the beginning of a one-way trip.

For emigrants heading to Oregon and California, the most popular way to pick up the main route—the Oregon and California Trails overlapped for the first 1,000 miles—was to travel to a jumping-off place along the Missouri River. These bustling towns were the last stops before the wilderness. Emigrants could pick up forgotten supplies, repair wagons, and hear the latest trail news. They could also join up with groups of other people heading into the unknown.

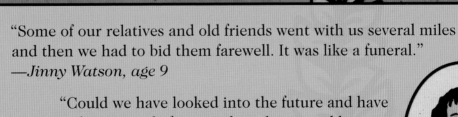

"Some of our relatives and old friends went with us several miles and then we had to bid them farewell. It was like a funeral." —*Jinny Watson, age 9*

"Could we have looked into the future and have seen the misery before us, these lines would never have been written. But we were full of hope and did not dream of sorrow." —*Virginia Reed, age 13*

WAGON TRAINS & HANDCART COMPANIES

Traveling in emigrant groups, called trains or companies, could have disadvantages. A group's leaders might be foolish or cruel. One person's poor choice could hurt everyone in the company. Each group created its own rules. Groups could choose to leave their members behind or kick them out if trouble arose. They might even choose to execute them. Each group also had its own prejudices. Some wagon trains did not allow African American emigrants to join. And disease could spread through traveling trains like fire through dry prairie grass.

But there were also benefits to traveling in a group. Young emigrants could make friends to play and do chores with. Families who traveled together often helped each other, especially when things went wrong. Mary Ann Stucki's family did not speak English when they made their journey. They relied on others in their handcart company to translate for them. When tragedy struck Catherine Sager's family, she and her siblings only survived because other families in their wagon train cared for them.

Emigrant groups could be huge. Owen Bush and Catherine Sager traveled in the same wagon train, but they may not have known each other. Their group had more than 300 people in it. But Catherine surely would have heard Owen's father play his bugle to wake everyone up in the morning.

Sometimes traveling with a group was more a matter of chance than choice. Elisha Brooks and his family traveled with several different wagon trains during their trip west. Sometimes they chose to leave a group, but other times they simply could not keep up.

Owen's father served as their wagon train's pilot. He was in charge of waking the group in the morning and finding new campsites. The family jumped off in May of 1844 and left the slave state of Missouri behind them forever.
—*Owen Bush, age 12*

"Our company were very fine people, perhaps one or two exceptions." —*Jinny Watson, age 9*

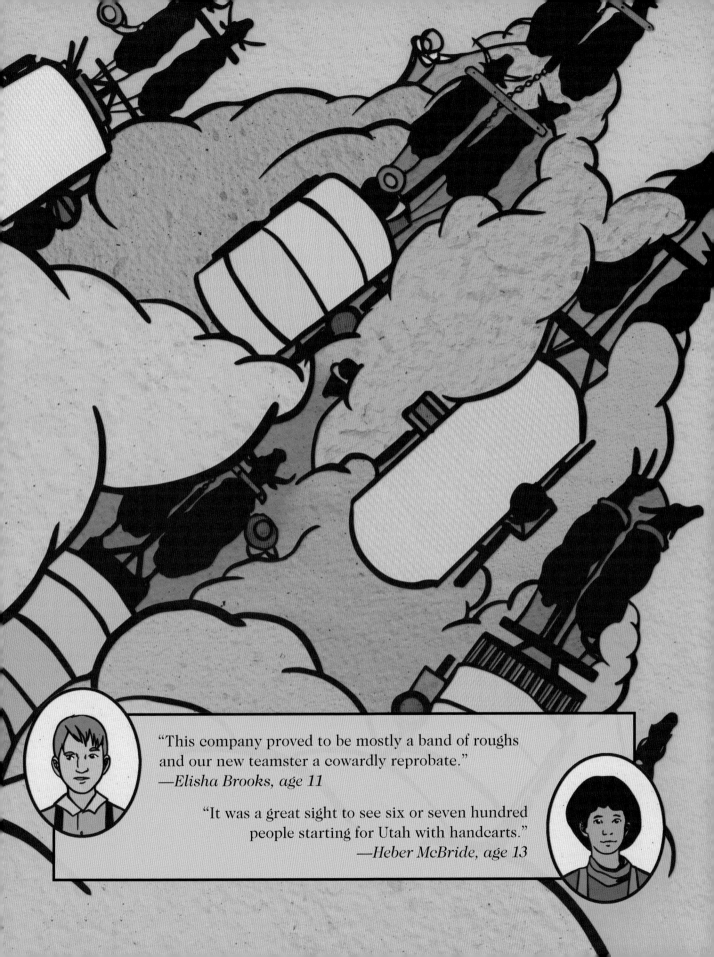

"This company proved to be mostly a band of roughs and our new teamster a cowardly reprobate."
—*Elisha Brooks, age 11*

"It was a great sight to see six or seven hundred people starting for Utah with handcarts."
—*Heber McBride, age 13*

TRAVELING

Most emigrants traveled west on foot. Walking made the wagon loads lighter and easier for the animals to pull. Sometimes, especially in bad weather, a traveler might retreat into the rolling wagon for a short break, but Prairie Schooners were uncomfortable. They were stuffed with supplies and bounced painfully over the uneven ground. The swaying of Catherine Sager's wagon made her feel sick to her stomach.

Walking was not exactly pleasant either. Young emigrants stumbled over sharp rocks and slipped on shifting sands. They picked their way through pricking cactus and drifts of freezing snow. When their shoes wore out, some emigrants traded with Native Americans for moccasins. Others went barefoot.

Some emigrants like Virginia Reed and Elizabeth Keegan were wealthy enough to have ponies to ride on the journey. Virginia Reed claimed that her mother's custom wagon was so comfortable, she could ride happily in it all day. But mostly, if people could walk, they did.

Eventually, young emigrants grew stronger and walking became easier. The soles of their feet became tough as leather and they had less trouble keeping up with their groups. Each wagon train and handcart company set their own pace and schedules. Owen Bush and Catherine Sager had to wake up at four in the morning, break camp at six, and roll out at seven exactly. The travelers had full days ahead of them. Walking was just the beginning of the work on the westward trails.

"On and on we journeyed—averaging fifteen miles a day over cactus, sage brush, hot sand! Everybody's shoes gave out and we bartered with Indians for moccasins, but that didn't help much about the prickly pears." —*Etty Scott, age 11*

"Breaking the way through the heavy sage brush was so hard on the lead team of oxen that their legs were soon bruised and bleeding, so each wagon had to take its turn at the head of the train for half a day, then drop to the rear." —*Benjamin Bonney, age 7*

"I rode through on horseback and I had a fine opportunity to see and examine everything of note on the way."
—*Elizabeth Keegan, age 12*

"I am wondering where we are. Day after day we travel and still we seem to be 'Nowhere' although the road is filled with teams. I wonder if any of them know where they are. No one appears to care." —*Harriet Hitchcock, age 13*

RESPONSIBILITIES

Young emigrants did a lot of work on the journey west. They helped their parents with hunting, cooking, sewing, babysitting, caring for animals, and whatever else they could manage. Virginia Reed helped her father scout for new campsites. Elisha Brooks and his twin brother drove their family wagon and kept watch at night.

"If you have ever tried to stop a runaway ox team you know what hard work it is." —*Benjamin Bonney, age 7*

Ellen Mason's mother, Biddy, was in charge of herding livestock, making and breaking camp, and cooking the group's meals. Ellen would probably have helped her mother with these tasks and looked after her two younger sisters. —*Ellen Mason, age 13*

One of the most important chores for young overlanders was gathering buffalo chips. These pieces of dried buffalo dung were odorless and burned remarkably well. Firewood was scarce in prairies and deserts. Sometimes buffalo chips were the only fuel for the family campfire. Young people raced to see who could gather the most chips or the biggest ones.

One responsibility most emigrants did not have on the trail was school. Some overlanders studied with their parents. But since there was plenty of other work to do, and there were not many books or teachers, school was usually postponed until the journey's end.

Back home, boys did some chores and girls did others. But on the trail, everyone pitched in however they could. Many girls stepped up to drive oxen or herd cattle. Some boys learned how to cook and sew. This was good practice for life in the West, where *what* you could do mattered more than *who* you were.

Young emigrants who lost a parent took on even more responsibility. They cared for the sick, parented younger siblings, and hunted for food. These young overlanders also made life and death decisions about where and how their families traveled.

"It was my duty to keep up the loose stock in crossing the plains, and I was given charge of an old Sorrel mare, who had one eye." —*Etty Scott, age 11*

Owen was old enough to share the wagon driving duties with his father. He may also have tended tiny tree saplings to be planted when the family reached the new country. —*Owen Bush, age 12*

RIVER CROSSINGS

On a map, the rivers that wove through the West looked as delicate as silken threads. In real life, their waters could be wide, wild, and deadly. Even their banks were treacherous. Deep mud sucked at wagon wheels and oxen feet. Pockets of quicksand dragged down unsuspecting horses and humans alike.

Emigrants might try to drive their wagons straight through shallow rivers. But crossing deeper water, they faced a real challenge: how to turn a covered wagon into a boat. If the water was calm, emigrants might take their wagons apart and float them across in pieces. Groups that could find trees sometimes built simple rafts and used ropes or long poles to guide them across the water.

Some crossing places had a ferry—boats or rafts that took people and wagons across the water—but they could be expensive. In 1850, crossing the Platte River on Hickman's ferry cost $5 per wagon—$164.35 in today's money. Most ferries charged extra for each animal, so cattle usually had to swim. But even ferries could not guarantee a safe crossing. Sallie Hester remembered that a "lady and four children were drowned through the carelessness of those in charge of the ferry."

Emigrants risked drowning and losing important supplies each time they crossed a river, but many families crossed time after time without trouble. Virginia Reed's servant Eliza Williams grew so used to crossing rivers, she barely noticed them. She once churned several pounds of butter as her wagon splashed across the Platte River.

"Crossed Truckee River ten times. Came near being drowned at one of the crossings. Got frightened and jumped out of the carriage into the water. The current was very swift and carried me some distance down the stream."
—Sallie Hester, age 14

"As the river remained high and there was no prospect of fording it, the men went to work cutting down trees, hollowing out logs and making rafts on which to take the wagons over."
—Virginia Reed, age 13

"We spent two days attempting various schemes for crossing, but the treacherous current and dangerous quicksands baffled all our efforts." —*Elisha Brooks, age 11*

"All of us were tucked inside the wagons; my father put me, last of all, inside that back end of the last wagon, told me to keep still and not be afraid." —*Etty Scott, age 11*

"Often the rain and snow was very disagreeable, but we were gradually becoming reconciled to it (at least we children were)." —*Jinny Watson, age 9*

"At about midnight we were awakened to find our tent blown down upon us, and our bed floating, while we, almost suffocated, were taking a bath somewhere in the interior." —*Elisha Brooks, age 11*

BAD WEATHER

The weather was another challenge of the trail. Bad weather could be uncomfortable and inconvenient. Or it could be deadly. Fierce winds ripped the covers off the wagons and made it almost impossible to put up tents. Snow and hail made everything cold and slippery. Rain soaked the emigrants to the skin and made it hard to stay warm and healthy. It seeped into stored food and made it mold and spoil. It drowned cookfires, made rivers flood, and turned the trails to oozing, spattering mud.

Spectacular thunderstorms rumbled across the plains, scaring animals and emigrants alike. Heber McBride was more impressed than frightened: "Iowa can beat the world for thunder and lightning, but I never was afraid of lightning." Thunder may not have bothered Heber, but it could scare cattle into a stampede.

Extreme temperatures could freeze or fry the emigrants. They might travel all night to avoid the noonday heat of a desert. Or sleep huddled together with their dogs to keep from freezing to death in the mountains.

Some bad weather had a positive side. Plenty of rain meant there was fresh water to drink and green grass for the grazing animals to eat. It kept down the choking dust churned up by hooves and wheels. And it fed the thousands of wildflowers that bloomed across the prairie.

Rough weather and harsh temperatures also made good weather something to celebrate. On mild days when the sun was shining and a fresh breeze was blowing, walking felt easier. Chores seemed to fly by. And that left more time for play.

"Even when it rained the company did not stop traveling. A cover on the handcart shielded the two younger children. The rest of us found it more comfortable moving than standing still in the drizzle." —*Mary Ann Stucki, age 6*

"We were kept awake last night by the constant roaring of thunder. It was truly terrific." —*Harriet Hitchcock, age 13*

FUN & PLAY

Young overlanders played whenever they could. They did not have many toys from home, so they made dolls out of grass and built dollhouses from buffalo bones. They kicked balls made out of rags or animal bladders. Cans and jars, strings and sticks—almost anything could become a toy.

Games were a great way to make new friends on the trail. All you needed for Anti-I-Over was a ball and a wagon. Two teams stood on either side of a wagon. Team One yelled, "Anti!" and tossed the ball over the wagon. If someone on Team Two caught the ball, they ran around the wagon and threw it at Team One. If they hit someone, the hit player joined Team Two. If no one was hit or Team Two did not catch the ball, a new round began. The game ended when one team had all the players.

"We put in three delightful days wading in the stream. It was October and the water was low. In many places there were sand and gravel bars." —*Benjamin Bonney, age 7*

"Swimming was the order of the day with all the small boys in the camp." —*Heber McBride, age 13*

Young overlanders also had climbing, shooting, and wrestling contests. They had ferocious buffalo chip fights and searched for swimming holes. They went exploring and watched birds, caught fish, and picked flowers. Sometimes they went hunting or tried to tame wild creatures.

Dancing was another way the emigrants, young and old, had fun. They whirled and stamped their feet to the sounds of fiddles and guitars. If no one had an instrument, the travelers could always sing. Even the smallest camps could be full of music.

"We had a merry time playing snowball and picking flowers in the snow." —*Harriet Hitchcock, age 13*

"There were several musical instruments among the emigrants, and these sounded clearly on the evening air when camp was made and merry talk and laughter resounded from almost every campfire." —*Catherine Sager, age 9*

CAMP LIFE

Camping out could be an incredible experience. Young emigrants danced and told stories by the fire. They watched spectacular sunsets over towering mountains, listened to lowing cattle bedding down for the night, and smelled the drifting scent of coffee and bacon in the crisp morning air. Unfortunately, battling hungry mosquitos and trying to cook in pouring rain were a part of camp life too.

A good campsite on the westward trails had things like nearby water, firewood, grazing for cattle, and game to hunt. But emigrants often settled for wherever they could stop safely before sunset. Pitching tents and lighting fires in the dark was a struggle no one looked forward to.

Once the animals were settled for the night, campfires blazed to life. Biscuits, bacon, and pickled or dried foods from home were a regular part of supper. The overlanders also ate fresh berries, fish, bear, buffalo, antelope, rabbit, and whatever other local eatables they could find.

Not everyone enjoyed the new foods. Virginia Reed thought the taste of buffalo was "excellent," but Jinny Watson "did not like the meat, it was dark and coarse." But even picky eaters were ready to dig in after a long day on the trails.

After supper was cleared away and everything readied for the next day, young emigrants might play, talk with friends, or relax a little around a campfire. When it was time for bed, overlanders who had wagons could sleep under them or even in them, if there was room. Other travelers slept in tents or outside under the starlit sky.

"When we camp at night, we form a corral with our wagons and pitch our tents on the outside, and inside of this corral we drive our cattle, with guards stationed on the outside of tents." —*Sallie Hester, age 14*

"At night the young folks would gather about the campfire chatting merrily and often a song would be heard, or some clever dancer would give us a barn-door jig on the hind gate of a wagon." —*Virginia Reed, age 13*

Evenings in camp were a good time to get to know other emigrants. Ellen and her family began to spend time with some of the free African Americans emigrants in their group. —Ellen Mason, age 13

"Ox yokes are not very good mattresses. There is not enough spring in them." —Elisha Brooks, age 11

EMIGRANTS & NATIVE PEOPLES

Many emigrants traded with the Native people they met on their journey west. Horses, warm furs, and fresh local foods were just a few of the important supplies they bargained for. Some of the foods were new to the emigrants. Benjamin Bonney remembered trying bread made of ground crickets and acorns. It "looked like fruitcake, but had a different taste."

Overlanders often depended on these trades to survive their journey, but many still treated the Native Americans they met with fear and disrespect. Most young emigrants had heard exaggerated, or entirely made-up, stories of what Native people were like. Many were terrified of being attacked on the trail. There were violent conflicts between Native Nations and overlanders, but most young emigrants never experienced one.

Emigrants, on the other hand, harmed Native people even when they did not intend to. They made a lot of noise as they traveled, scaring away the wild animals Native Americans hunted for food. Emigrant cattle ate huge amounts of grass, leaving little for those Native Nations, like the Sioux, who depended on grazing animals like horses and buffalo. The emigrants used up important water sources and dirtied others with their laundry, bathing, and animals.

The overlanders also spread sickness as they traveled. Native Americans had no immunity to emigrant illnesses. During a smallpox outbreak in Oregon in 1853, about half of the Native people living in the lower Columbia River region died of the disease.

"We had learned that [the white man] brought goods whenever he came and that our people exchanged furs for his merchandise." —*Ohiyesa, Santee Sioux, age 8*

"We suffered vastly more from fear of the Indians before starting than we did on the plains." —*Virginia Reed, age 13*

"The people that my grandfather called our white brothers came along to where our winter supplies were. They set everything we had left on fire . . . It was all we had for the winter."
—*Thocmetony, Northern Paiute, age 10*

"The emigration of '47 brought the measles among the Indians and great numbers of them died. I have known five to be buried in one day." —*Catherine Sager, age 9*

"I fell out of the wagon, the wheels passing over me broke one leg very badly." —*Catherine Sager, age 9*

"The mare began to plunge and I soon saw she was in quicksand. I held on tightly to her rein, yelled with all my might, knowing there was a man behind me also driving stock. He heard me and rushed to my assistance."
—*Etty Scott, age 11*

ACCIDENTS & MISTAKES

The most common accidents for young emigrants were wagon related. Playing around the heavy Prairie Schooners was dangerous. One missed step or snagged piece of clothing, and a young overlander could easily end up under a wagon's crushing wheels. Other accidents were caused by carelessness or risky choices. Emigrants tripped down rocky slopes and stumbled into boiling springs. They wandered too far from camp and got lost. Sometimes they were even left behind. Catherine Sager's older brother tried to start a campfire using gunpowder. Thankfully, he only lost his eyebrows when it exploded.

Even a carefully considered choice could turn out to be a deadly mistake. Cutoffs were a tempting gamble on the journey west. These shortcuts promised to save emigrants time and miles, but they were not always what they seemed. Benjamin Bonney took a cutoff that brought him safely to California. But the cutoff Virginia Reed and her family took led them to utter disaster.

Virginia's group, the Donner-Reed party, wasted weeks on Hastings Cutoff. On a map, the shortcut saved emigrants 300 miles. In reality, the rough trail went through steep hills and parched salt flats. It was harder and slower to travel than the main route. Dangerously delayed, the group reached the Sierra Nevada Mountains late in the year and were trapped in winter snow. Faced with starvation, the desperate emigrants ate their cattle, their dogs, their boots, and, eventually, their dead.

Miraculously, Virginia's entire family survived the infamous tragedy. Writing to her cousin after her rescue, Virginia had very specific advice for those who wanted to travel west: "Never take no cutoffs and hurry along as fast as you can."

"I never saw better pasture than we had after leaving the main traveled road." —*Benjamin Bonney, age 7*

"Took a cutoff; had neither wood nor water for fifty-two miles." —*Sallie Hester, age 14*

HUNGER & BAD WATER

Even with careful planning, emigrants could run out of food or water. Sometimes their supplies were lost or destroyed. Other times food ran out because the overlanders got stuck.

Insects, drought, snow, and too many travelers could destroy the plants the oxen and mules grazed on. If the animals pulling the wagons did not get enough to eat, they grew weak and eventually died. Emigrants who lost their teams had to buy or trade for new animals. If they could not, they had to abandon their wagon and keep moving as best they could. Stranded overlanders quickly used up the limited supplies they had with them.

When Heber McBride's handcart company was stranded by a snowstorm, they began to reduce each family's food ration. By the time fresh supplies arrived, Heber's family was surviving on a few ounces of flour a day. Their combined flour rations were not enough to make bread, so they boiled it in water with oxen bones to make a thin soup.

Most wagons carried at least one cask of water to refill at streams and rivers. But sometimes the water sources the travelers counted on were dried up. Other times, earlier emigrants had drunk them dry or dirtied them. Desperate oxen and humans alike could die from drinking bad water.

Not getting enough food or water quickly weakened emigrants. It made it easier to fall behind. Or get sick.

"The oxen one by one fell by the way; some wagons were abandoned." —*Etty Scott, age 11*

"We made our last cup of flour into flapjacks and ate our last slice of bacon, then lay down to a hungry sleep." —*Elisha Brooks, age 11*

"My two little brothers would get the sack that had flour in and turn it wrong side out and suck and lick the flour dust off it." —*Heber McBride, age 13*

"There is a well here, but the water is so poor we cannot drink it. But we are getting accustomed to live without water." —*Harriet Hitchcock, age 13*

SICKNESS & DEATH

Sickness killed more young people on the westward trails than accidents, hunger, and bad weather combined. Measles, scurvy, scarlet fever, typhus, and mountain fever took many lives. Cholera—an infection causing vomiting, cramps, and diarrhea—was the worst of all. In 1850, it killed 2,000 emigrants. Some victims died within a few hours of becoming sick.

Many wagon trains could not, or would not, wait for someone to recover from an illness. Families had to choose between moving with the group and staying behind to care for their sick loved one. Some tried to do both, tending to the sick person in the dark rattling wagon as best they could.

BELOVED MOTHER

"So in twenty-six days we became orphans. Seven children of us, the oldest fourteen and the youngest a babe." —*Catherine Sager, age 9*

"Often we saw a company stopped by the roadside burying one of their fellow travelers or perhaps one of their family. We had very little sickness and not one death in the company." —*Jinny Watson, age 9*

Without wagons, Heber McBride and his sister struggled fiercely to keep their weakening parents moving westward: "We would find Mother lying by the side of the road first, then we would get her on the cart and haul her along till we would find Father lying as if he was dead. Then Mother would be rested a little and she would try and walk and Father would get on and ride."

Not everyone suffered from disease. Jinny Watson and Elizabeth Keegan saw the ravages of cholera along the trail, but their families managed to stay healthy. Sallie Hester's mother actually felt better on the trail than she had at home. Others were not so lucky.

Heber never knew if it was hunger or cold that finally ended his father's life. He only knew that the loss broke his heart. Cholera took Etty Scott's mother and a fever took her brother. Catherine Sager's father died of "a species of the camp fever." Her mother followed within a month.

"A man was taken ill and his cries of agony drove sleep from many a pillow that night." —*Elizabeth Keegan, age 12*

"The passing of that dear, beloved mother was a crushing blow to all our hopes." —*Etty Scott, age 11*

GOING ON

Thousands of people lost their lives traveling west. Just like today, those still living came together to help each other grieve and keep going. Overlanders shared their wagons, oxen, food, and clothes. They took in orphans. Many recovered from their illnesses and injuries thanks to the care of their friends and family. Heber McBride's mother overcame her exhaustion, "chills and fever." Catherine Sager's leg healed.

Emigrant families pushed each other onward. They asked each other to go a little farther, walk a little longer. Some reconsidered what was important. The trail was littered with prized possessions the travelers decided were worth less than their lives. As Elisha Brooks recalled, "we cast aside everything but the absolute necessities; we exchanged our wagon for a lighter one that we found abandoned—we had our choice of many—and wondered when the end would come and what the end would be."

Despite the sorrows and the dangers, there were still things to be thankful for on the westward trails. Many young emigrants reached their destinations with new siblings. They made new friends and playmates. Sometimes an entire wagon train would stop to celebrate a wedding or the Fourth of July.

For the emigrants heading to Oregon and California, the final push over the mountains could be the toughest one. The weather was cold, the trail was steep, and everyone was exhausted. In some places the mountainsides dropped away so sharply, the wagons had to be lowered down with ropes. But when emigrants reached the other side, the trails ended, and brand-new journeys began.

"I realized that I must be strong and help mama bear her sorrow."—*Virginia Reed, age 13*

"Among the young children to be taken to Oregon was my sister, Ellen Francisco, who had been born at Sutter's Fort and who was only a few months old."
—*Benjamin Bonney, age 7*

"We journeyed on, amid hardships that to any of your generation would seem impossible." —*Etty Scott, age 11*

"To look forward was to look directly upwards as the ascent seemed nearly perpendicular, but remembering our motto 'perseverance' we doubled our teams and went on." —*Harriet Hitchcock, age 13*

"When we came to Ft. Walla Walla we saw a crowing rooster on a rail fence. Oh, how we all cried. It was a sweet sound to our ears. There we stood, travel worn, weary heart and homesick group, crying over the sound of a rooster crowing."
—*Etty Scott, age 11*

"Standing there at the end of a twenty-eight-hundred-mile journey, through the most inhospitable part of our country . . . thrilled us with a joy for which there is no language."
—*Elisha Brooks, age 11*

TRAIL'S END, NEW BEGINNING

After months of hard traveling, young emigrants stepped off the westward trails and into new lives. The joy of finally reaching their destinations could be overwhelming. They had made it! But the trail's end was not the same for everyone.

Native people like Thocmetony and Ohiyesa continued to endure extreme and destructive changes to their traditional ways of life. But they did not disappear. More than five million Native Americans live in the United States today.

When Owen Bush's family finally arrived in Oregon, they were in for a shock. While they were traveling, the Oregon Provisional Government had passed a law forbidding African Americans from settling in the Oregon Territory. The family had to build their new life in what is now Washington state instead.

For Elisha Brooks, whose father had traveled west two years earlier, reaching California meant that his family was finally together again. Orphans like Catherine Sager, however, had to make their way in the West without their parents' help.

Enslaved people like Ellen Mason should have been free as soon as they entered states where slavery was illegal. But many slave owners refused to let their slaves go. Ellen's mother took their master to court and won freedom for her children and for herself.

The end of the journey west was just the beginning for young emigrants. Their lives stretched out before them. There were crops to plant and homes to make, cities to build and communities to shape. As Sallie Hester remarked, they were "strangers in a strange land—what will the future be?"

"After we got down into the valley all our difficulties were at an end. We met houses at every turn of the road and flourishing farms, called here, ranches." —*Elizabeth Keegan, age 12*

Despite the prejudice they continued to face in the West, Owen's family started a 640-acre farm. It was very successful. The Bushes often shared their crops with needy neighbors and helped other new emigrants start their own farms. —*Owen Bush, age 12*

What Happened to the Young Emigrants?

All of the young people featured in this book really lived. Each of their stories could fill its own book, but here is a little more about who they were and what their lives were like out West.

 **Benjamin Bonney**—Benjamin was seven when his family set out for the West in 1845. The Bonneys settled briefly in California, but moved to Oregon a year later when the Mexican-American War began. Benjamin's family settled on land with plenty of trees and he spent a lot of time making and selling cedar shingles for houses. When he grew up, Benjamin worked as a carpenter, bricklayer, miner, and eventually a preacher. He was married three times and had nine children.

 **Catherine Sager**—Catherine's trip west was a tragic one. Traveling in 1844 when she was nine, Catherine and her siblings were orphaned on the Oregon Trail. Members of her wagon train brought Catherine to a new family in Washington, but she was orphaned again in 1847 when her adopted parents died in a conflict with members of the Cayuse Nation. Catherine and her surviving sisters were sent to live with different families in Oregon, but kept in touch. She eventually settled near Salem, Oregon, where she and her husband ran a large farm and raised eight children.

 **Elisha Brooks**—Elisha was eleven when he traveled west. He set out with his mother and siblings in 1852 to join his father in California. Unfortunately, Elisha's mother never recovered from the hard journey and died five years later. Elisha worked all sorts of jobs to make ends meet. He drove oxen and sold wildflowers. He served in the Civil War and even worked for the U.S. Mint. Eventually, Elisha became a teacher. He had never had much time or opportunity to go to school himself, but Elisha spent more than twenty years working in San Francisco schools.

 **Elizabeth Keegan**—Elizabeth was twelve in 1852 when she made her journey to California. At first, she had mixed feelings about her new home. She missed the friends she had left back east. She also missed her little brother and sister who had stayed behind in St. Louis. They joined her in California two years later. Despite her early feelings, Elizabeth stayed in California for the rest of her life. She married, had two children, and ran a boarding house there.

 **Ellen Mason**—Ellen made two trips on the western trails when she was enslaved. She traveled from Mississippi to Utah in 1848 at age ten, and from Utah to California in 1851, at thirteen. In 1856, Ellen's mother, Biddy Mason, took their master to court and won freedom for herself and her family. Ellen's mother became a tremendous community leader and real estate businesswoman. Ellen shared her mother's dedication to helping others and worked to improve the lives of African Americans in Los Angeles, the state of California, and the nation.

Etty Scott—Etty traveled across the country in 1852 when she was eleven. Though her mother and one of her brothers died on the trail, Etty made it to the West with her father and seven other siblings. Three of her siblings became newspaper editors and journalists, but Etty's story of her journey west was not published until after her death. Etty married twice and had two children. She "lived to see two great cities grow from a few pioneer cabins—Portland, Oregon, and Seattle [in Washington]."

Harriet Hitchcock—When Harriet's father headed to Colorado to look for gold in 1864, thirteen-year-old Harriet, her sisters, and her mother went with him. Harriet and her family returned to their eastern home a few months later, but Harriet was not finished with the West. After attending college, she married and moved—by train—to Oregon in 1883. She and her husband had two children and eventually settled in California.

Heber McBride—Herber and his family left their home in England to travel the westward trails in 1856. Sailing across the Atlantic Ocean on a huge ship was thirteen-year-old Herber's favorite part of his long and difficult journey to Utah. He and his handcart company left too late in the year and became trapped in a snowstorm. At least 150 people died, including Heber's father. Heber grew up to be a soldier and a farmer. In 1866, he helped rescue another group of emigrants stranded along the Platte River, close to where his father was buried.

Jinny Watson—Nine-year-old Jinny and her family had excellent luck on their trip west in 1849. As she remembered, "the loss of our horses was the worst trial that we met with on that long journey." When they arrived in Oregon, Jinny's uncle and cousins, who had emigrated the year before, helped the new arrivals get on their feet. Jinny's family set up a homestead near Salem, Oregon. She went to the very first school built there.

Mary Ann Stucki—Mary Ann was only six when her family left Switzerland to travel the Mormon Trail in 1860. They spoke very little English when they made their journey. Her handcart company encountered little trouble on the trail and her family settled in southern Utah. Mary Ann grew up and married, but was widowed only two weeks later. After marrying her second husband, she moved to Nevada, where she raised a large family and was a beloved member of her church community.

Ohiyesa—When Ohiyesa was four, he survived the Sioux Uprising of 1862, a violent conflict between his people and the emigrants and government of the United States. Ohiyesa spent the next ten years living a traditional Santee Sioux life, but when he was fifteen, his father convinced him to adopt the ways and customs of the emigrants. Ohiyesa changed his name to Charles Eastman and attended European-style schools, but maintained his traditional beliefs. He grew up to become a doctor, author, lecturer, and activist for Native American rights.

Owen Bush—Owen was twelve when his family traveled west in 1844. Despite facing racism and the harsh challenges of the trail, Owen's family was incredibly generous to their fellow overlanders. They paid for wagons and supplies for at least two other emigrant families. Owen's family could not settle in Oregon because of its Black Exclusion Laws, so they built a thriving farm in Washington instead. Owen became a talented farmer and was elected to the state's House of Representatives. He worked to pass laws promoting agriculture and racial equality. A butternut tree his family brought across country is still growing where they planted it 170 years ago.

Sallie Hester—Fourteen-year-old Sallie enjoyed a peaceful journey west in 1849. Her family faced very little hardship and even her mother's carpet made it safely to California! Sallie kept a diary on the trail which revealed a lot about what daily life was like for overlanders. Her first winter in the West was not a happy one. Sallie hated the rain and the snakes and wanted to go back to Indiana. But once her family settled in San Jose, California, Sallie started school and began to make friends.

Thocmetony—Thocmetony, or Sarah Winnemucca as she was later called, was a member of the Northern Paiute Nation and was born in what is now Nevada around 1844. In 1865, her mother was killed by the Nevada Volunteer Cavalry. Sarah spoke several Native American languages as well as English and Spanish, and worked as an interpreter between her people and the U.S. government. She traveled all over the country, speaking and advocating for better conditions and rights for her people. Her autobiography *Life Among the Piutes: Their Wrongs and Claims* was the first book published by a Native American woman.

Virginia Reed—Thirteen-year-old Virginia and her family were part of one of the most infamous disasters on the westward trails. In the winter of 1846, the Donner-Reed party spent months trapped by snow in the Sierra Nevada Mountains. Virginia recalled, "certainly no family ever started across the plains with more provisions or a better outfit for the journey; and yet we reached California almost destitute." After they were rescued, the Reed family settled in San Jose, California. Virginia wrote two accounts of her journey west. The first was published when she was just fourteen. Virginia grew up to become a successful insurance and real estate businesswoman, and raised nine children.

A NOTE FROM THE AUTHOR

This book is not nearly big enough to tell you everything that happened on the westward trails. Instead, it is my hope that it will serve as your own personal jumping-off place and that you will journey on to learn more. Hundreds of books have been written about the Westward Expansion and the people affected by it. Ask your local librarian to recommend one, or two, or ten!

All of the people featured in this book really lived. The quotes I have included are from the diaries, letters, and published stories they left behind. Spelling and grammar in the 1800s were pretty terrible. For clarity, I have changed most of the spelling and grammar in the quotes to what we would use today.

The two African American emigrants featured in this book, Owen Bush and Ellen Mason, are not quoted. Though many enslaved and free African Americans went west by covered wagon, stories written in their own words are rare. Stories written by African American emigrants younger than fifteen are even rarer. Ellen Mason and Owen Bush appeared in newspapers and the diaries and trail memoirs of other emigrants. Their stories were also passed down orally through their families. African American emigrants like Owen and Ellen helped shape the West, and their stories are important. Although I cannot quote them, I have included them to the best of my ability.

Many of the young people in this book changed their names as they grew up, married, or changed religions. I have used the names or nicknames they would likely have had at the ages I have listed. To assist you in your exploring, I include their full names here:

Benjamin Bonney (Benjamin Franklin Bonney); Catherine Sager (Catherine Sager Pringle); Elisha Brooks; Elizabeth Keegan (Elizabeth Keegan Ketchum); Ellen Mason (Ellen Mason Owens Huddleston); Etty Scott (Harriet Louise Scott McCord Palmer); Harriet Hitchcock (Harriet Adelle Hitchcock Lucus); Heber McBride (Heber Robert McBride); Jinny Watson (Virginia Watson Applegate); Mary Ann Stucki (Mary Ann Stucki Reber Hafen); Ohiyesa (Charles Alexander Eastman); Owen Bush (William Owen Bush); Sallie Hester (Sallie Hester Maddock); Thocmetony (Sarah Winnemucca Hopkins); Virginia Reed (Virginia Bakenstoe Reed Murphy).

I am deeply indebted to the Oregon Historical Society and the many passionate trail historians and scholars who have come before me. Thank you especially to Lee Kreutzer, Cultural Resources Specialist/Archeologist at the National Park Service, for offering invaluable expert feedback on the manuscript. I would also like to gratefully acknowledge the following for their kind permission to reproduce quotes by Heber McBride, Sallie Hester, Virginia Reed, Etty Scott, Elizabeth Keegan, and Harriet Hitchcock in this book:

Best of Covered Wagon Women, Volume II: Emigrant Girls on the Overland Trails edited by Kenneth L. Holmes and published by University of Oklahoma Press, 2010.

M MSS 501; Heber Robert McBride autobiography; 19th Century Western & Mormon Manuscripts; L. Tom Perry Special Collections, Harold B. Lee Library, Brigham Young University.

Thank you also to the incredible creatives who contributed their insights, suggestions, and encouragement to the creation of this book—Chamisa Kellogg, Heidi Aubrey, Kaaren Pixton, Barb Kerley, Anne Broyles, Ellen Howard, and Emily Whitman. I would especially like to thank fellow author Elizabeth Rusch for her enduring mentorship, friendship, and infectious passion for nonfiction. I'd also especially like to thank my husband, Travis. This book would not exist without your love and support. Thank you!

SOURCES

ARTICLES

Ayer, John E. "George Bush, the Voyageur." *The Washington Historical Quarterly*. Vol. 7, No. 1 (January 1916), pp. 40–45

Bonney, Benjamin F., Lockley, Fred. "Recollections of Benjamin Franklin Bonney." *The Quarterly of the Oregon Historical Society*. Volume XXIV (March, 1923 - December, 1923), pp. 36–55.

"Death of Donner Party Members." *The Californian*. February 18, 1921. rb.gy/dpnxhv.

Dunn, Jewell L. "Nobody Actually Knows What George Bush Looked Like – DNA attempts to tell us the story." Out of the Archives, October 2016.

Hedges, Andrew H. "When Men and Mountains Meet: Pioneer Life in Utah's Ogden Valley." *Mormon Historical Studies* 2, No.2 (Fall, 2001), pp. 115-134.

Millner, Darrell. "George Bush of Tumwater: Founder of the First American Colony on Puget Sound." *Columbia Magazine*, Vol. 8, No.4 (Winter 1994-95), pp. 14-19.

Murphy, Virginia R. "Across the Plains in the Donner Party: A Personal Narrative of the Overland Trip to California." *Century Magazine*, Volume 42 (July, 1891).

"Pioneer of Polk and Marion Dead." *The Capitol Journal*, March 20, 1923. rb.gy/z80so9.

"Raymond Resident, In Salt Lake In 1856, is Claimed By Death: H.R. McBride is Extolled at Funeral Service – In Raymond since 1904." *The Lethbridge Herald*, August 5, 1925. rb.gy/ypuydz.

Richardson, Sarah. "Freedom Trail." *American History*, December 2018. Gale Academic OneFile. Accessed June 1, 2020. rb.gy/fk636m.

BOOKS

Beasley, Delilah L. *The Negro Trail Blazers of California: A Compilation of Records from the California Archives in the Bancroft Library at the University of California, in Berkeley; and from the Diaries, Old Papers, and Conversations of Old Pioneers in the State of California.* Los Angeles: Times Mirror printing and binding House, 1919.

Brooks, Elisha. *Elisha Brooks: The Life-Story of a California Pioneer: Written for His Grandchildren to Show Them how the Emigrants Crossed the Plains, and Also what Manner of Person was Their Great Grandmother.* San Francisco: Abbot-Brady Printing Corporations, 1922.

Campbell, Marne L. *Making Black Los Angeles: Class, Gender, and Community, 1850-1917.* Chapel Hill: University of North Carolina Press, 2016.

Dary, David. *The Oregon Trail: An American Saga.* Oxford: Oxford University Press. December 8, 2005.

Eastman, Charles A. *Indian Boyhood.* New York: McClure, Phillips & Co, 1902.

Fitzgerald, Michael O. "Preface." In *The Essential Charles Eastman (Ohiyesa): Light on the Indian World*, edited by Michael Oren Fitzgerald, Bloomington: World Wisdom, 2007.

Hafen, Mary A. *Recollections of a Handcart Pioneer of 1860.* Lincoln and London: University of Nebraska Press, 2004.

Hastings, Lansford W. *The Emigrants' Guide to Oregon and California 1845: Containing scenes and incidents of a party of Oregon emigrants : a description of Oregon : scenes and incidents of a party of California emigrants, and a description of California, with a description of the different routes to those countries, and all necessary information relative to the equipment, supplies, and the method of traveling.* Cincinnati: George Conclin, 1845.

Hester, Sallie. "The Diary of a Pioneer Girl 1849," in *Best of Covered Wagon Women, Volume II: Emigrant Girls on the Overland Trails*, edited by Kenneth L. Holmes, Norman: University of Oklahoma Press, 2010.

Hitchcock, Harriet. "Thoughts by the Way 1864-1865," in *Best of Covered Wagon Women, Volume II: Emigrant Girls on the Overland Trails*, edited by Kenneth L. Holmes, Norman: University of Oklahoma Press, 2010.

Hopkins, Sarah Winnemucca. *Life Among the Piutes: their wrongs and claims*. New York: G.P. Putnam's Sons of New York, 1883.

Keegan, Elizabeth. "A Teenager's Letter from Sacramento 1851," in *Best of Covered Wagon Women, Volume II: Emigrant Girls on the Overland Trails*, edited by Kenneth L. Holmes, Norman: University of Oklahoma Press, 2010.

Moore, Shirley A. W. *Sweet Freedom's Plains: African Americans on the Overland Trails, 1841–1869 (Race and Culture in the American West Series)*. Norman: University of Oklahoma Press, 2016.

Murphy, Virginia R. "The Donner Party Letters 1846," in *Best of Covered Wagon Women, Volume II: Emigrant Girls on the Overland Trails*, edited by Kenneth L. Holmes, Norman: University of Oklahoma Press, 2010.

Murphy, Virginia R. "Virginia Reed Murphy (1833–1921)." In *Unfortunate Emigrants*, edited by Johnson Kristin, 262-86. University Press of Colorado, 1996.

Palmer, Harriet S. "Crossing Over the Great Plains 1852," in *Best of Covered Wagon Women, Volume II: Emigrant Girls on the Overland Trails*, edited by Kenneth L. Holmes, Norman: University of Oklahoma Press, 2010.

Unruh, John D., Jr. *The Plains Across: The Overland Emigrants and Trans-Mississippi West, 1840-60*. Urbana and Chicago: University of Illinois Press, 1993.

Werner, Emmy E. *Pioneer Children on the Journey West*. Boulder: Westview Press, 1995.

West, Elliott. *Growing Up with the Country: Childhood on the Far Western Frontier*. Albuquerque: University of New Mexico Press, 1989.

ONLINE SOURCES

Boyd, Robert. "Disease Epidemics among Indians, 1770s-1850s (essay)." The Oregon Encyclopedia. Accessed June 1, 2020. rb.gy/kf21mm.

"Bridget 'Biddy' Mason." National Park Service. Accessed June 1, 2020. rb.gy/nmmco2.

"Bush Butternut Tree." Bush Prairie Farm. Accessed June 1, 2020. rb.gy/ksz9uz.

Caldbick, John. "Bush, William Owen (1832-1907)." Historylink.org. August 2, 2013, rb.gy/ziygzh.

Campbell, Robert L. "[Journal extracts, 30 June-19 Oct. 1848], in Historian's Office, Journal 1844-1997. The Church of Jesus Christ of Latter-Day Saints. Accessed June, 1, 2020. rb.gy/en0mcx.

"Crossing the North Platte River." WyoHistory.org. April 25, 2016. rb.gy/gocptl.

"Ellen Mason." The Church of Jesus Christ of Latter-Day Saints. Accessed June 1, 2020. rb.gy/8djtzy.

"George and Isabella Bush, Tumwater Pioneers." Bush Prairie Farm. Accessed June 1, 2020. rb.gy/ahpoid.

"George Washington Bush and the Human Spirit of Westward." U.S. National Park Service. February 1999. rb.gy/xpokvj.

Hill, William E. "Prairie Schooner." Britannica. Accessed June 1, 2020. rb.gy/urb51g.

"Historical Trails: Trail Basics – The Wagon." National Oregon/California Trail Center. Accessed June 1, 2020. rb.gy/a6shmk.

"History and Background of Pioneer Bush Family." City of Tumwater. July 6, 1945. rb.gy/ymoyuv.

"The 'Independent Colony' over the Trail to Oregon." Start-wa.com. Accessed June 1, 2020. rb.gy/5svuzy.

Jefferson, Alison R. "Pioneering Black Urbanites in San Francisco and Los Angeles." California Historical Society. February 4, 2019. rb.gy/sj7pq2.

Nokes, Greg. "Black Exclusion Laws in Oregon." The Oregon Encyclopedia. Updated March 17, 2018. rb.gy/t27nof.

Olsen, Winnifred. "William Owen Bush (1832-1907)." Black Past. September 25, 2018. rb.gy/lexmq4.

Peterson, Paul H. "They Came by Handcart." The Church of Jesus Christ of Latter-Day Saints. August, 1997. rb.gy/8mzhjt

"Tribal Nations and the United States." National Congress of American Indians. February, 2020. http://www.ncai.org/about-tribes.

Ziontz, Lenore. "George and Isabella Bush: Washington's First Family." City of Tumwater. Updated July 18, 2005. rb.gy/gc910c.

PRIMARY SOURCES

Applegate, Virginia W. Recollections, [manuscript] ca. 1900. Mss 233, Oregon Historical Society Research Library.

McBride, Heber R. M MSS 501; Heber Robert McBride autobiography; 19th Century Western & Mormon Manuscripts; L. Tom Perry Special Collections, Harold B. Lee Library, Brigham Young University.

Pringle, Catherine S. Catherine Sager Pringle Papers, Mss 1194, Oregon Historical Society Research Library.

THESES

Andros, Jill Jacobsen, "Children on the Mormon Trail" (1997). All Theses and Dissertations. 4481. https://scholarsarchive.byu.edu/etd/4481.

Edited by Michelle McCann
Layout by Jane Damiani

Library of Congress Cataloging-in-Publication Data

Names: Goss, Elizabeth Ames, 1987- author, illustrator.
Title: My way west : real kids traveling the Oregon and California trails / by Elizabeth Goss.
Other titles: Real kids traveling the Oregon and California trails
Description: [Berkeley, California] : West Margin Press, [2021] | Title from cover. | Includes bibliographical references. | Audience: Ages 7-10 | Audience: Grades 2-3 | Summary: "Based on real letters and memoirs, 'My Way West' presents true historical stories and experiences from kids on the Oregon and California Trails in the mid to late 1800s"— Provided by publisher.
Identifiers: LCCN 2021001640 (print) | LCCN 2021001641 (ebook) | ISBN 9781513267302 (hardbound) | ISBN 9781513267319 (ebook)
Subjects: LCSH: Overland journeys to the Pacific—Juvenile literature. | Pioneer children—Overland Trails—Juvenile literature. | Pioneers—Overland Trails—Juvenile literature. | Oregon National Historic Trail—History—Juvenile literature. | California National Historic Trail—History—Juvenile literature. | Overland Trails—History—Juvenile literature. | West (U.S.)—History—1848-1860—Juvenile literature. | Frontier and pioneer life—West (U.S.)—Juvenile literature. | Wagon trains—West (U.S.)—Juvenile literature.
Classification: LCC F593 .G67 2021 (print) | LCC F593 (ebook) | DDC 978/.02—dc23
LC record available at https://lccn.loc.gov/2021001640
LC ebook record available at https://lccn.loc.gov/2021001641

Proudly distributed by Ingram Publisher Services

Printed in China
25 24 23 22 21 1 2 3 4 5

Published by West Margin Press®

WEST
MARGIN
PRESS
WestMarginPress.com

WEST MARGIN PRESS
Publishing Director: Jennifer Newens
Marketing Manager: Angela Zbornik
Project Specialist: Micaela Clark
Editor: Olivia Ngai
Design & Production: Rachel Lopez Metzger

ELIZABETH GOSS is an illustrator, author, and professional papercutter. She has a passion for history and loves poking through old books in dusty libraries. Elizabeth lives in Portland, Oregon with her husband and cat. To learn more about Elizabeth and her work, please visit lizabethgoss.com.